T0078150

"SUPEREROGATION" AGAINST "ARROGANCE"

CHARLENE KLING

authorHOUSE®

AuthorHouse™
1663 Liberty Drive
Bloomington, IN 47403
www.authorhouse.com
Phone: 1 (800) 839-8640

Published by AuthorHouse 11/06/2015

ISBN: 978-1-5049-5842-4 (sc)
ISBN: 978-1-5049-5841-7 (e)

Print information available on the last page.

Preface

This story is for those of you whom work for others but never ask for anything in return.

This is also dedicated to those that have past.

This also stories of nurse assistants and what they go through while working and how they handle it.

I am introduce the first part of my story for my friend Diane, myself and Diane have been friends since we first started working together as certified nurse assistants. Diane continued on to be a LPN.

The health field will always need nurses and certified nurse assistants.

When Char asked me to add a fee things to her stories, I was honored.

Nurse Assistants are severly under-rated. They do the job that no-one else wants to do. There are so many things that nurse assistants have to put up with. I think the #1 Thing is short staff!!!! I bet you who are in nursing understand this. It seems like administration department heads are always adding more duties than one person can do.

Lets take a typical 1st shift. You arrive at 6am get report then have anywhere from 10 – 17 patients to take care of before breakfast by 7:15am. This is extremely hard in a nursing home if there is more then one of these patients to get up by hoyer lifts. (hoyer lifts are mechanical lifts to get patients up one by one). Of course there are patients that can do themselves. In assistant living places is usually they can do there selves. Sometimes you are working so hard you do not get a break or lunch.

One night, Diane, and one of our co-workers, went to check on two lady's,

The co-worker had just come back from vacation. The one lady said,"Where have you been?" The co-workers told her, "I went to see my sister!' and, she said, "Oh! I thought you died and gone to hell!" To this day we all laugh about it. Another night all of us were putting clothes away for the patients room's. Our friend and co-worker came out of a room slapping her chest, and breathing heavy. We thought she was having one of her asthma attack's. She came running down the hall, and we followed her she kept slapping her chest she finally yelled," There is a mouse in the closest!"

she opened her blouse, and the mouse jumped on the floor we finally caught it. It wasn't funny at the time, but we all laughed about it the next day. When Diane, and myself, and another co-worker well all were talking about what we couldn't clean up, well Diane said, "I hate cleaning up vomit!" and the co-workers said," I don't like cleaning up blood!", and I just sat there listening shaking my head, I thought to myself that is a certain ow-man they are asking for trouble, it was a full moon, what could happen will probably happen.We all continued with our rounds checking on the residence, our co-worker went down the hall, she went into the last room to start with her rounds. One of the lady's in the room was vomiting, and the other one was chewing on her fingers and there was blood everywhere. That night I helped them clean up both residence with both co-workers, I thought we was going to clean more vomit.

Another night there was a co-worker that kept us all laughing. We would be on our break, and she would start imitating Beavis," I am cornholio! I need T.P for my bunghole."

She always be there when I needed someone to cheer me up if I had a bad night. Otherwise none of us would make it through the night.

It takes a very special person to be in the health field be it from being a nurse assistant up to being a doctor. **You have to be dependable, and honest, patient, compassionate, loving. And respectable.**

When your a nursing assistant you have to be strong, and no back problems. Its to withstand all the lifting you have to do.

You have to have a good heart, and be able to walk away if you are hit, bitten or kicked.

You can't take all these abuses personally. Sometimes these are the only way for the patients to lash out at the world. You have to look at these things as a communication tool sometimes for them. Also if they have Alzheimer they do not what they are doing. I think the hardest thing a patients point of view is when you still have your mind, but can't anyone what they need.

It must be very frustrating. Try to put yourself in that person's place what would you do?

How would you handle that problem?

When I was a nursing assistant I would think of different ways to communicate those patients.

Being in the health field, and taking care of patients know matter what field your in can be hard, and also be rewarding. I myself have had those days where I just want to throw in the towel, and say,"To hell with this, I can't take anymore!"and leave, but something always keeps me going, and coming ba I think the worse is when someone steals from a patient. These people who come into these Assistant living homes or nursing homes have had everything taken from them. Homes, furniture, and most of the independence from them. How can anyone stoop so low as to take something from someone? I will never understand that. How would you feel?

I know of a couple of workers in different places, they were fired, and went to jail. But still its the way they make the patient feel insincere after that, so you have to made they feel secure after that happens.

The other thing that rates in my, "horrible list!" has to do with some family members that I have run into I can't imagine putting your mother or father in a home and never going to see them, or to tell the nurse not to call unless the they are dying. That actually happened, and I was shocked., So was the nurse that took the call. Her and I went outside on a break together, and cried for the patient.

How can anyone be so greedy, and cruel.?

So, all of you out there, don't think the nurses, and nursing assistants are the bottom of the cookie jar, they are the heart of it . They are the eye's, and ears of the health field, and deserve the utmost respect for what all of them do.. If you would like to become a nursing assistant, or nurse, go for it. It can be very rewarding, and fulfilling career if you have the heart or stamina for it, I salute all the nurses, and nursing assistants.

Nursing Assitants and What it Means!

What is a nursing assistant? Well she, or he, is someone that is there when a friend, or a relative is in the hospital, nursing home, and assistant living homes, or helping with hospice, or home health aide. They are the eye's, and ears of the nurses, so they know what is going on, and to tell them how the patients are, or also if they have past away.

When I started work I would get to know the patients, or residence myself, that is a good thing to do first if the patient, or resident is new, and even when not its nice to let them know you will be activities, if they are in a good mood, or not.

If the patient is in the last stages of there Alzheimer's you want to find out how they are doing on that day.

One of the hardest things to walk in on is if the patient has past away. It takes a minute to get your bearings sometimes, then let the nurse know stat. (which means right now)! After the nurses, and physicians have took notes, and all they have to do, you have to put it in the computer to what time, and all you have to so it is on record..

The next thing we have to do is get the patient cleaned up for the family. I always try to get to know my patients, or resident to see if they can walk, happy, or sad, see they are inconstant, or needs a wheelchair. To know them its easier to care for them.

One night I went to answer a light, and the person cannot talk only a little. The only way she can communicate is by writing a note. It was really hard to see her cry because she's in a nursing home, and she is only 40.That is really young to be in there. I hate to see young people in those facilities. Anyways I helped this lady up, and she had me call her daughter for her. Later that evening, her daughter came to see her. It was nice to see her smile.

You see, nursing assistants do have compassion. The good ones, I know everyone has heard of the bad stuff we do, but there are more good ones then bad ones.

Diane, and myself have been letting others know what to expect if they ask what it is like so we are letting all of them know what we have been through.

Family that is where everything starts from helping each other, and our parents.

You see, if you hear all the things we go thru you won't know what its like until you see or go thru it yourself.

My husband didn't know what I did at work until we were taking care of his mother, we had her at our house later in her cancer. His mother was a great lady, but when they get sick its hard for them to ask for help. Like when they have to get cleaned up of help get dressed. Hospice is a God sent! I knew what to expect, but my husband did not. He finally said,"This is what you do at work?" Right then he realized how hard my job could be. What was really hard is to find his mom had past away. It is always is hard know matter if your a nursing assistant or, anyone else it is always hard to see someone has past away.

I don't think anyone knows how hard it is until they go thru it themselves. In 1997, it helps when your a nursing assistant, and helping family. I was working 3rd shift at the time, my had cancer. I would stop by, and have a cup of coffee with my mom, and dad. For a while my mom would do a lot of things herself, I was glad because, anyone that is sick, or with cancer it makes them feel better.

She felt bad when I helped her, I just told her to think of when she helped me when I was at home or younger, and am helping you because I want to. Hospice came into the home to help with my mom, it made dad happy to keep her at home. My brother, and I, along with our family lived next to them in our homes. We came over, and helped our dad with my mom, and anything else we could do.

My mom had breast cancer, and was in her bones also. She was sicking in a chair with family **around (she had lost a lot weight) he bones were brittle, we went to get her up, and we heard herbones crack, it was a horrible sound. We got a hold of her cancer doctor, they got her a special bed** unfortunately she went into a nursing home they could take care of her, the special bed had a rotating sand to make sure she did not get bed sores, and help with her bones.

My mother was a special lady, she did not complain or yell, she loved everyone. We would come visit her all the time, I would go, and help the nurse assistants take care of her as much as I could. I guess I went more because it made my dad feel better if he left for a while. When she got further along in her sickness she would tell me to make sure my father was okay after she past, it made me uncomfortable, but I listened to her.

One morning I showed up before my dad, and she was talking very faintly, my father showed up after he showed up, she past away. I still miss her today. After my mom past away we found out that our father had lung cancer, and his was into his bones also. My brother, would take turns going over to take care of him. I have 3 older brothers.

I lived closes to my brother Dave, and Doug lived about 20 miles away, our other brother lived in Arizona at the time, he felt bad because he couldn't make it while our dad was sick, I just explained to him that our dad understood.

Some people would complain because he was still smoking he just told them the damage is done so he was going to smoke as long as he can. He got weak he fell at home, he was taken to grand rapids hospital, they wanted to hook him up to a feeding tube, I told my brothers it would take a court order to take it out, know one explained that to my dad, so I went in and explained it to him, he said he wanted to go home. He was happy to be at home. It wasn't to long after that, that he went into another hospital.

He past away. I miss him also to this day, it was 5 months apart that my mother, and father past away.

Nursing assistants have to be ready for any personality, and the outcome of how a patient feels.

Like, some patients can't walk, and they blame everyone around them. There is always a way to cheer them up, or at least make them feel a little better, for example find out from family what he use to like, or books, \just try to find out about the person, and forget the personality, because if you dwell on the bad frame of mind, your not any better, and one thing I learned is grin, and bare it.

I have worked in different nursing homes, and living assistant homes, and even tried factory work. I would stop, and see my parents on the way home from work, my dad use to ask me, "where are you working now!" I guess I always had reasons going from job, to job. I even had people harass me for it. I didn't care what anyone thought, I guess I needed to find myself at the time, I talked to my dad about it, he always told me not to settle, to do what is best for yourself.

Then when I started to help take care of my mom I quit work for a while to help my dad to take care of my mom, she was more important. When I would go over in the morning to have a cup of coffee with my mom, and; dad, they would joke with me, and told me I should write a book, I have written one, but this is personal to my family, and my friends.

After being around helping both my mom, and dad, I guess I just new being a nursing assistant was what I wanted to do. I've been asked,"what do think about your job when you go home?" Good nursing assistants would sometimes wonder if they remembered certain things, To vent about bad things I talk to my friend Diane, she knew what I was going through of course you don't say names, but it is good to talk to someone who has been there.

This is my spouse Dennis is was in the Navy, and proud of it, and grandson Thomas, and of course myself.

Palliative Care/Veterans Administration

I started working as a nursing assistant, at the veterans administration in 2001. On my first day my director of nursing told me not to get to close to the veterans on this floor, because they won't be here long, because of cancer. (Of course I thought what a thing to tell a nursing assistant, it's hard not to get close to themselves patients) When I started to get to know the veterans they were so happy to talk to someone, they knew they were sick, but most of them didn't dwell on it. I did get close to the veterans I took care of, I new what I would find some day, but I didn't think about it, as long as I could help, and listen to there stories, and make them happy that is all that matters. What is really bad is when you go into a room, and find someone had past away. It really hurts, but you think of all that you did with the veteran, helping, listening, and that is all good. I think they past away feeling relieved. I worked for palliative care for 4 years, I found out I was allergic to the latex gloves. I was transferred to patient service assistance, I am still working with the veterans so I was really happy, I worked at Battle Creek Michigan for 8 years. I transferred to Traverse City Michigan the clinic for the veterans administration, because we moved to Mesick Michigan. I worked there for 5 years when I was in a serious car accident. After the accident I received a certificate in creative writing, I have a published book, and this is about helping

the nursing assistant stories, and to tell all

the stories here are true. I want to Thank

those I have worked with, and family, and

especially Diane my friend.

Printed in the United States
By Bookmasters